The Student's
TOOLBOX

TIPS FOR BETTER RESEARCHING

LOUISE SPILSBURY

Please visit our website, www.garethstevens.com. For a free color catalog of all our high-quality books, call toll free 1-800-542-2595 or fax 1-877-542-2596.

Library of Congress Cataloging-in-Publication Data

Spilsbury, Louise.
Tips for better researching / Louise Spilsbury.
    pages cm. -- (The student's toolbox)
Includes bibliographical references and index.
ISBN 978-1-4824-0160-8 (pbk.)
ISBN 978-1-4824-0158-5 (6-pack)
ISBN 978-1-4824-0159-2 (library binding)
1. Study skills. 2. Research. 3. Students--Life skills guides. I. Title.
LB1049.S697 2014
371.30281--dc23

2013028173

First Edition

Published in 2014 by
Gareth Stevens Publishing
111 East 14th Street, Suite 349
New York, NY 10003

© 2014 Gareth Stevens Publishing

Produced by Calcium, www.calciumcreative.co.uk
Designed by Emma Debanks and Paul Myerscough
Edited by Sarah Eason and Ronne Randall

Photo credits: Cover: Shutterstock: ImageryMajestic. Inside: Dreamstime: Americanspirit 10, Bradcalkins 9, Georgiana Branea 1, 11, Lisafx 13, Santos06 8; Shutterstock: 28, Andrey Popov 18, David Ashley 15, Blend Images 16, Jacek Chabraszewski 4, Hung Chung Chih 17, Dtopal 19, Jcjgphotography 25, Karelnoppe 29, Kazoka 24, Denis Kuvaev 26, MatteoNannelli 7, Michaeljung 20, Martina Osmy 22, Nenov Brothers Images 23, I. Pilon 6, Takayuki 5, Toranico 27, Udaix 21, Mattomedia Werbeagentur 12, Feng Yu 14.

Printed in the United States of America

CPSIA compliance information: Batch #CW14GS: For further information contact Gareth Stevens, New York, New York at 1-800-542-2595.

CONTENTS

Chapter One: What Is Research? 4

Chapter Two: Starting Out.. 6

Reading and Brainstorming.. 8

Primary and Secondary Sources... 10

Choosing Books.. 12

Finding Your Way Around Books 14

Chapter Three: Searching the Internet... 16

Choosing Websites Carefully.. 18

Chapter Four: Filtering Information.. 20

How to Take Notes... 22

Organizing Your Notes 24

Showing Your Sources 26

Chapter Five: Using Your Research.. 28

Glossary... 30

For More Information.. 31

Index 32

CHAPTER ONE

WHAT IS RESEARCH?

What do you or your family do before you buy an expensive item such as a phone or a computer? You research! You find out about the different models available and how much they cost before you make a purchase. Research is an important life skill. Being able to find and use relevant information helps you make choices, reach conclusions, and communicate well.

Find Out More

When people are researching an important purchase, they don't use just one source of information to discover what they need to know. They may ask friends, look on the Internet, and read reports in newspapers, magazines, and sales catalogs. They check different, reliable sources and make notes so that they can make a decision based on all of the information they find. That's what you need to do in preparation for reports and projects. You need to research by gathering information from a wide variety of reliable sources, before coming to a conclusion or figuring out a final plan.

We research to get information, such as which bicycle is best for rough terrain.

Research can help you figure out how to tackle a tricky assignment!

Researching Well

Good research helps you produce good projects. Research skills enable you to find information in different places. Reading this book and discovering better research skills will help you to:

- Know how to plan a research project.
- Learn how to carry out a research project.
- Find out how to use informational books, encyclopedias, and other useful library books.
- Improve the way you use the Internet for research.
- Learn how to read through sources quickly to find the information you need.
- Discover the best way to take notes and organize them.

A BOOK OF IDEAS

TIPS FOR SUCCESS

Keep a small notebook and a pen with you at all times. If you read or overhear something that might be useful for your project, or ask someone a question while you're away from your desk, you can then write it down so you don't later forget it.

STARTING OUT

The first step toward great research is to be clear about what information you're going to look for before you start. If you can choose your own topic, choose one that really interests you. That way you'll enjoy working on it more. If you are researching a school project, you'll usually be given a subject to work on. Be sure to understand what type of project you are going to work on to help you research the correct information.

Collect the Right Material

Different types of projects require different types of information. Check that you understand what you're being asked to do before you begin researching, so you can collect the right material from the start.

- Informational essays require information from books, journals, and other sources.

- Posters require drawings and photographs.

- Reports about an event in the past or an opinion piece may benefit from quotes, to help explain events firsthand.

- PowerPoint presentations require images and possibly video clips.

- A local history project requires interviews with family, friends, or other local people.

How about researching old maps for a history project?

You could narrow a broad topic about deserts to one on only desert animals.

Read the Title

Reading the title of a research project might seem obvious! However, it is important to look out for the key words in the title. These are the words that tell you important parts of the project:

- Compare and contrast: This means you should describe similarities and differences among things.

- Describe or outline: This means you should explain the main facts about the subject in question.

- Discuss: This means you should give the pros and cons of opposite sides of an argument.

- Justify or explain: This means you should say how and why something happens, using examples and evidence.

- Demonstrate or show: This means you should give examples to prove something.

BREAK IT DOWN

Sometimes you may be given a broad topic title for a research project, such as "Ancient Rome." This is a large, complex topic, so it might help to focus on one feature of it. Instead of writing about "Ancient Rome," you could look at "Daily Life in Ancient Rome."

TIPS FOR SUCCESS

READING AND BRAINSTORMING

When you are given a new research topic, you'll probably already know a little about it, unless it's a wacky story title such as "Describe Life as an Alien on the Planet Grark!" Before you start working on your project, you need to think about what you already know and do some background reading to find out even more.

Brainstorming

Brainstorming helps you discover what you already know about a topic. To brainstorm:

- Sit down with a pen or a computer and write whatever comes into your head about your topic, even if you think it's wrong.

- Write down as many ideas as you can, without stopping, in around three to five minutes.

- Don't worry about spelling, grammar, or neat writing as you write down your ideas.

When you read through what you've written down, you may have some useful ideas that can be developed for your research project.

Brainstorming releases all the bright ideas in your head!

8

Building a Background

It's a good idea to gather some background information about your topic before you begin your research. An encyclopedia is a great place to find background information. Encyclopedias have short entries that give you a useful overview of most subjects. They are usually arranged alphabetically and have guide words at the top of every page to help you find the right entry. You can use this information to build up a list of key words to help with your research. For example, if an encyclopedia tells you snakes are a type of reptile, you can research the word "reptile" as well as "snake."

PICTURE THIS!

You could make a spider diagram or mindmap to note some of the things you already know about your topic from brainstorming and background reading.

TIPS FOR SUCCESS

PRIMARY AND SECONDARY SOURCES

You're ready to start researching and you want to use a variety of sources, but which different sources should you look at and what are the differences between them? Sources used for research are usually divided into two groups, primary sources and secondary sources.

Primary Sources

Primary sources are original, firsthand accounts or evidence about a person, place, object, or an event. The account might be from someone who experienced an event. It might be from a person who knew the person you wish to write about. Primary sources are records of something that happened, was said, or thought about at one point in time. Examples of primary sources include letters, photographs, diaries, videos, interviews, autobiographies, and speeches.

A soldier may be able to give a firsthand account about a war.

Secondary Sources

Secondary sources are secondhand accounts. They are written or created by people some time after an event. They explain, comment on, or draw conclusions from primary sources. Examples of secondary sources include textbooks, history books, and encyclopedias. Newspaper and magazine articles can be primary or secondary sources. If the article was written when something happened or just afterward, it is a primary source. If a reporter writes about an event in the past, using information written by someone else, it is a secondary source.

Newspaper articles can be primary or secondary sources.

It's All About Trust

Secondary sources are easier to find than many primary sources. However, it is important to use reliable secondary sources—ones you can trust. To discover if a secondary source is reliable:

- Find out who wrote the secondary source—are they trustworthy?
- Discover if the author used evidence to support his or her ideas.
- Check that the author has an obvious opinion about the topic.

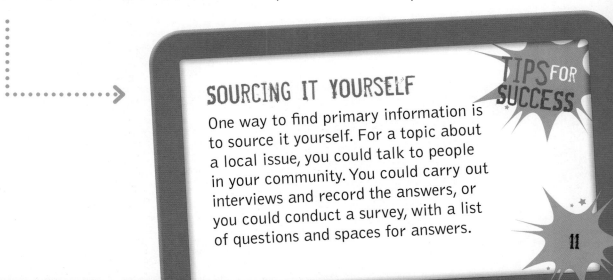

SOURCING IT YOURSELF

One way to find primary information is to source it yourself. For a topic about a local issue, you could talk to people in your community. You could carry out interviews and record the answers, or you could conduct a survey, with a list of questions and spaces for answers.

TIPS FOR SUCCESS

CHOOSING BOOKS

Books are an excellent place to start your research because they have been researched, checked, and edited by professional writers and publishers. If you choose the right books, they can provide reliable and interesting information. How do you go about choosing which books to read?

Reference and Informational Books

Reference books include dictionaries, atlases, and encyclopedias. Informational books usually focus on one topic or subject, such as animals, volcanoes, or world religions. Reference books are a great way to find reliable information about your topic. One of the advantages of reference books is that they are carefully selected by librarians. Librarians are experts at choosing good quality, reliable books and they have probably found resources about your topic for other students before.

Library reference books are an ideal source for research.

Librarians can help you use a database to find a particular book.

How to Find Books in a Library

A library can have hundreds or even thousands of books.
What is the best way to find the books you need?

- Browse the shelves. Books are usually divided into subjects, such as sports and history. Use the divisions to help you find your topics.

- Use the library catalog—this is usually a computer that is easy to use. You can search for the name of the book, the author, or the subject you need.

- Ask library staff to help you find information. Most librarians will go out of their way to help you.

CHECK IT OUT

Remember, you cannot believe everything you read just because it is in a book! You can be more certain that a fact is correct if you read it in several sources.

TIPS FOR SUCCESS

FINDING YOUR WAY AROUND BOOKS

When you leave the library with a large stack of books, research might not seem like such a great idea after all! How will you find the time to read every page of all those books? The good news is, you don't have to. Books have features such as indexes and chapters to help you quickly find the information you need.

Cut to the Contents

Informational and reference books usually begin with a table of contents. This is a list of the parts of the book, organized in the order in which they appear. The table helps you find your way around the text inside. It usually includes the titles of the chapters or sections in the book and tells you on which page they start. Let's say you pick up a book about whales of the world, but your project is about humpback whales. You should be able to use the contents list to go straight to the relevant section without reading any of the other pages.

The contents page is always at the front of a book, where we begin to read the text.

Contents

Contents ....

Notices ....

Safety information

About this

Some indexes also tell you which pages have pictures of your research subject.

Getting into an Index

An index is another useful tool for quickly finding your way around a book. You'll usually find the index at the back of informational and reference books. It is a list of all the important parts and topics of the book and is arranged in alphabetical order. If a whale book doesn't have a separate chapter about humpback whales, simply go to the index. Look in the list of entries under the letter "H" to locate the pages where there is a mention of humpback whales.

FINDING ILLUSTRATIONS

Indexes can also help you find illustrations, photographs, maps, or diagrams. In some indexes, you will see page numbers in italics, such as *112* or *16*. This means there will be an illustration about the subject on that page.

TIPS FOR SUCCESS

15

SEARCHING THE INTERNET

The Internet is another good place to carry out research, but there is a vast amount of information on the World Wide Web. There are well over 150 million websites and some are made up of hundreds of thousands of web pages! The Internet is an online library of endless primary and secondary sources, so where do you start?

Search Engines

You can use search engines such as Yahoo!, Bing, or Google to find out about a subject. To use a search engine, type the topic you are searching for into the search box and click on "search." You will get better results if you type more than one word into the search box—if you want information about penguins, don't just type in "birds." Try to be more specific.

The Internet is great for research if you use it properly.

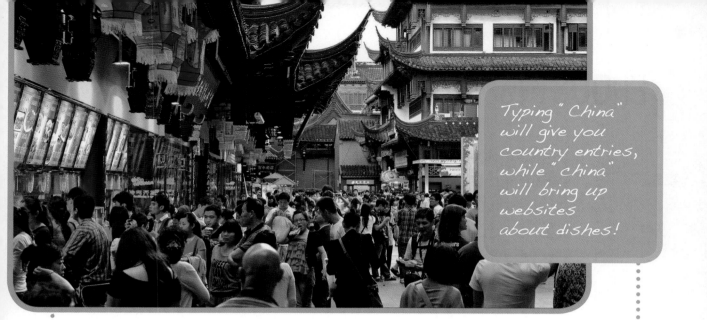

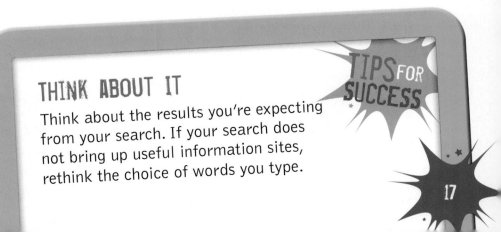

Typing "China" will give you country entries, while "china" will bring up websites about dishes!

Search Engine Suggestions

Try these suggestions to improve your Internet searches:

- Avoid writing complete sentences when you are searching. Use key words instead, such as writing "bears," rather than "Where can I find information about bears?"

- Check your spelling. Most search engines will search for exactly what you have written down.

- Use quotation marks. If you're looking for a short phrase or two to four words that go together, put them in quotation marks, such as "polar bear."

- You can search for one word and exclude another by using a minus sign. For example, to search for whales, but not blue whales, you would type "whale -blue."

- If one set of words does not bring up the right information, try different ones. For example, instead of searching for "soccer scores," try the key words "soccer" and "results."

THINK ABOUT IT

Think about the results you're expecting from your search. If your search does not bring up useful information sites, rethink the choice of words you type.

TIPS FOR SUCCESS

CHOOSING WEBSITES CAREFULLY

In a library, you can check who wrote a book, who published it, and when. This can tell you how reliable or trustworthy a book is. When using the Internet it's not always easy to tell who wrote or uploaded the information, so how can you carefully choose the websites you select for research?

Reliable Sources

Anyone can post information on the Internet, so every search you carry out will give you a range of reliable and unreliable results. Some of the information you find will have been carefully put together by experts or teachers. However, some will have been put together by unqualified people who may not have checked the facts they mention. One easy rule to remember is to look for websites that end in .gov (which stands for government), or .edu (which stands for education), or .org (which stands for organization). These "domain names" tell you that the site has been made by a trustworthy organization.

Look for websites written by experts.

University websites are written by well-informed people who are studying the subject.

Check Your Checklist

When you find a website, work through this checklist before you use the information:

- Check if the website has a modern design. Up-to-date, well-designed sites are usually reliable.
- Check if the facts match up with what you already know. If they do not, the site may not be reliable.
- Check who wrote the information. If the website does not state who wrote the information, the author is unlikely to be an expert.
- Check when the information was uploaded. Reliable sites are usually updated regularly.
- Check if the information gives only one opinion. If so, it may be biased.
- Check if the information contains advertisements. If so, the people who created it are probably trying to sell you something.
- Check if the site can be edited by anyone. If so, it may not be trustworthy.

INTERNET-LINKED BOOKS

Some informational books will provide ideas about where to look for more information on the Internet. These are called Internet-linked books. This means that they suggest websites you can explore to help you with your topic.

TIPS FOR SUCCESS

FILTERING INFORMATION

Skimming and scanning may sound like activities you would do at the beach, but they are in fact very useful research skills! They help you to find information in various sources, when you do not have time to read through everything.

Scanning

Scanning means flicking your eyes over a text to find specific words. People use this technique to find information such as dates, names, things, and places. If your project is about vitamins, you could scan over the pages of a food book, looking only for the word "vitamins." To scan effectively:

- Take your time—if you scan too quickly, you might miss key words.

- Look only for the first few letters of a word, instead of the whole word.

- On a website source, click on the "find" option and choose key words. The computer then scans for you!

Scanning helps you spot the main ideas of a text.

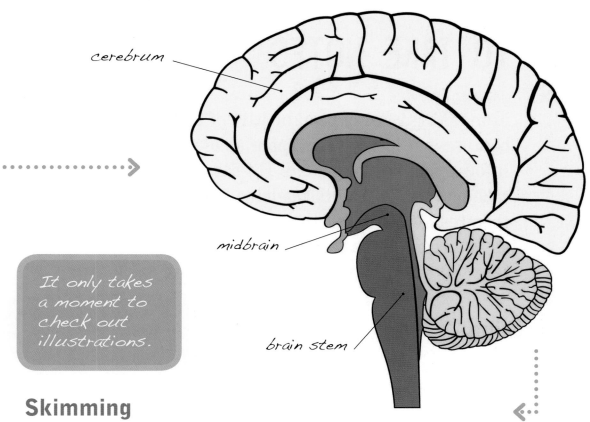

cerebrum

midbrain

brain stem

It only takes a moment to check out illustrations.

Skimming

Skimming is a way of reading a page of text to find the pieces of information that are useful, without reading every word. To skim a page, you look only at certain parts of the text. To skim:

- Read the title, the introduction or first paragraph, and the final paragraph of a long chapter. This will provide an overview of the information that chapter contains.

- Look at all of the titles, headings, and subheadings on a page and any words that are in bold or italics. This will help you find any material that is important.

- Look at the illustrations, photographs, charts, and graphs. These quickly tell you what the text is about, and these images will also help you understand the subject.

FACT BOXES

Look out for fact boxes—they usually tell you important information about a topic.

TIPS FOR SUCCESS

HOW TO TAKE NOTES

Note-taking is an important part of research because it helps you remember all of the information you have read. The best way to take notes is to read through the text once, then read it again but this time taking notes as you read. There are several different ways to take really great research notes.

Paraphrasing

When you rewrite what you've read in your own words, it is called paraphrasing. This helps you understand what you are reading and focus on the points that relate to your project. You can check the original text to copy important spellings correctly. You can also look up words you don't understand in the glossary, so you can explain them in your notes.

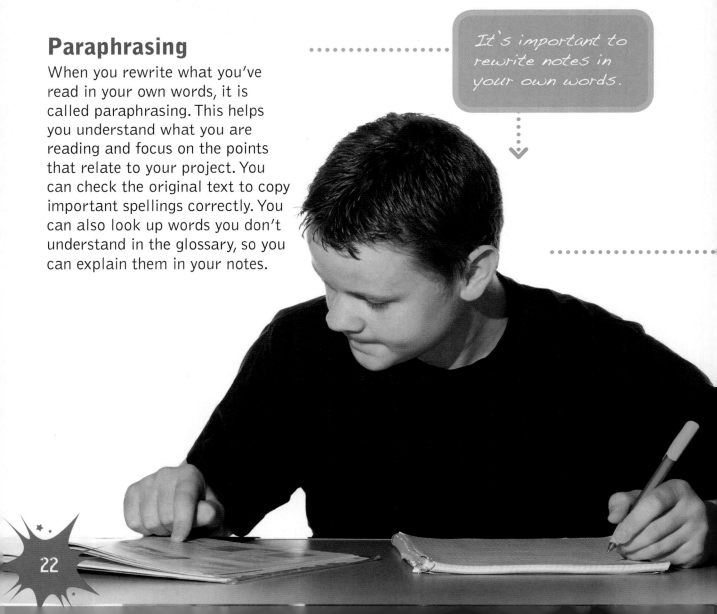

It's important to rewrite notes in your own words.

Nutrition

Nutrition (also called no...
aliment) is the provision...
organisms, of the mate...
(in the form of foo...
Many common hea...
...ted or allev...

You can highlight useful pieces of text on photocopied pages from a book.

Summarizing

Summarizing is when you note down only the key points from a text, such as important dates, events, people, and places. A summary is usually much shorter than the original text. To summarize a text, read it through once or twice and then write down the main points, without looking at the text again. Use bullet points instead of full paragraphs and keep the sentences short.

Highlighting and Marking

Highlighting pages you have photocopied or printed out from the Internet is useful only if you also add your own notes and comments to them. To do this, use a highlighter pen when you first read through the text. Mark any areas of text or words that are relevant to your assignment. Then, when you read through the text for a second time, write notes in the margin. Use your own words to summarize or paraphrase the highlighted text, or to explain how it might be useful.

QUOTING PEOPLE

If you copy something directly from a book without putting it into your own words, put quotation marks around it. This shows that it is an exact quotation.

TIPS FOR SUCCESS

ORGANIZING YOUR NOTES

When you think you've completed your research, it's time to start organizing your notes in preparation for writing your assignment. Hopefully, you have found lots of interesting information during your research, but how can you now organize it?

Sort It Out!

A good way to start organizing your notes is to sort your information into different categories or groups. First, take a few minutes to think about all the information you've gathered and decide what the main points are. You could organize the information chronologically, which means sorting it according to when things happened. You could also group it by different ideas. For example, if you've been researching a project about lions, you might have a set of notes that you can sort into groups such as: "where lions live," "what lions eat," "how lions hunt," "lion cubs," and "threats to lions."

You can use different colors to sort different themes.

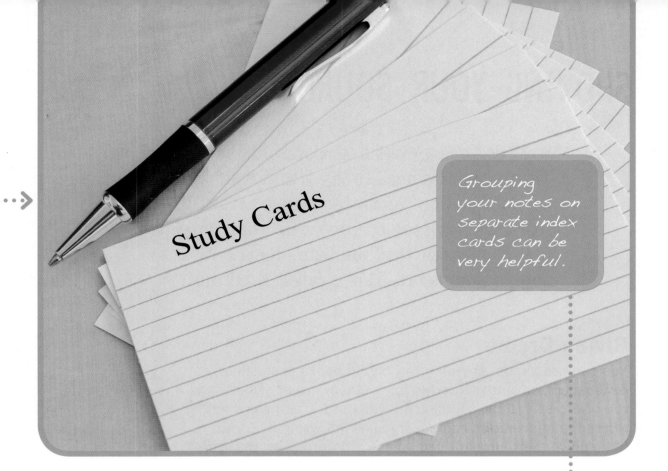

Study Cards

Grouping your notes on separate index cards can be very helpful.

Note Cards

You can sort your notes into lists on paper, onto a word document on your computer, or on note cards called index cards. Put a list of headings on a page or document or on individual index cards. Try to keep to one idea per heading or per card. If you have a card called "What Lions Eat," you can put all the information you've gathered about that topic on that card, or under one heading. Grouping notes in this way helps you compare the facts you have found. This helps you to spot mistakes, such as two sources that say different things.

BRIGHT IDEAS

TIPS FOR SUCCESS

Index cards are very useful because they can be easily grouped together or rearranged. Try to make note headings clear, or even highlight them in a different color. This will make it easier to sort through your notes when it is time to write your report.

SHOWING YOUR SOURCES

What do you say when someone gives you something? Thank you! You need to say "thank you" when you use information from other people's work. Their work will have helped you write your project, so it is only fair that you thank them with a note in your work. This is called "crediting."

Giving Credit

You can use almost anything you find in books, magazines, newspapers, or on the Internet for a school project, as long as you give credit to the sources that you used. That means noting where the information came from and who wrote it. Try to write down the source for each piece of information that you find while you're researching a project.

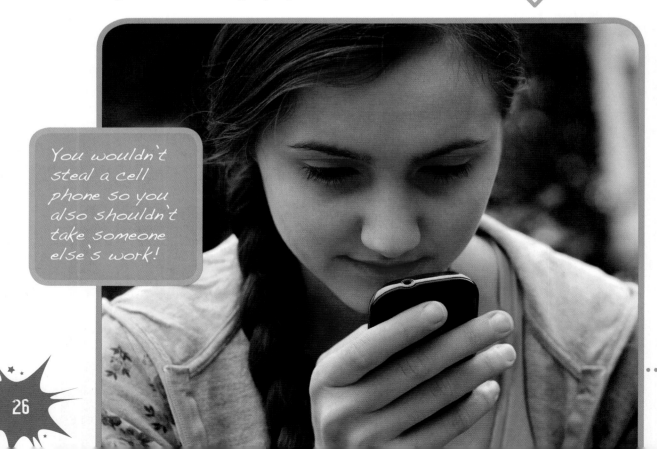

You wouldn't steal a cell phone so you also shouldn't take someone else's work!

SAVE YOURSELF TROUBLE

TIPS FOR SUCCESS

Another good reason to record your sources is so you can easily find them again. If you know where your notes came from, you'll have no trouble finding the book or website that the information came from once more.

Citing Sources

People usually put a list of their sources at the end of a book or project. This list is called the bibliography. In books, the bibliography is usually written in alphabetical order by the author's last name. To write your bibliography:

- Include the title of the source, the author, publisher, and place and date of publication.
- An online source should include the title of the website and the URL address, such as The Trail of Tears: www.pbs.org/wgbh/aia/part4/4h1567.html

Avoiding Plagiarism

Citing your sources is an important way to avoid plagiarism. Plagiarism is when a writer uses someone else's words or work and claims that it is his or her own work. Plagiarism is a form of cheating. Some students copy other people's words by mistake and do not mean to cheat, but this can still get students into trouble.

Teachers can easily discover plagiarism by typing a sentence from a suspected piece of plagiarism into the Internet.

27

USING YOUR RESEARCH

If actors learn their lines for rehearsals, their show should go well, and if a team practices before a match, they stand a much better chance of winning it. Good preparation helps us do something well, so good research and good notes should help you produce a better piece of work.

Thinking It Through

When you have created a set of well-organized notes, you are ready to create an outline. An outline shows your ideas and the order in which you are going to write about them. To write your outline, first read or skim through your notes to remind yourself of everything you have learned. This will help you get an overview of the information and help you figure out a plan.

When your research is finished, it's time to start writing.

Setting Up a Sequence

A good set of notes is vital for writing an outline. If your notes are organized into groups or themes, all you then have to do is put them into a logical sequence. Decide which parts of the research information should come first and which should follow. If your notes are grouped on index cards, just shuffle the cards until you have an order you are happy with.

Use Your Research

Remember, you did a lot of hard work during your research—don't waste it! Take this chance to show off some of the most interesting pieces of information you have discovered. Write the information as best you can, and try to add some images and quotes to make it really stand out. Make your project an example of how great research leads to great work!

Better research helps you produce work that makes you feel proud!

29

GLOSSARY

accounts reports or descriptions of events or experiences

articles written works published in print or on the Internet

atlases books of maps or charts

autobiographies accounts of people's lives written by those people

brainstorming trying to solve a problem by thinking intensely about it

bold describes letters on a page that have thick, heavy lines

comment to explain or remark on something

communicate to exchange information or opinions with another person

compare to describe the similarities between things

complex not easy to understand

conclusions final parts of an argument or text

cons disadvantages

encyclopedias books that give information on many subjects or on many aspects of one subject

evidence facts and information collected to support things we say

experts people with special knowledge

focus to concentrate and listen well

grammar rules about language and the way we write

journals newspapers or magazines that deal with a particular subject

opinion a personal view, idea, or judgment about something

professional created by someone trained or skilled in an area

pros advantages

relate to connect to

relevant related or connected to

reliable trustworthy

reports written accounts

research investigation into something

sources books or documents used to provide evidence in research

specific particular or precise

subheadings secondary headings underneath a main heading

survey an investigation of people's opinions by asking them a set of questions

topic a subject or theme

vitamins substances found in some foods that are good for us

FOR MORE INFORMATION

BOOKS

Asselin, Kristine Carlson. *Smart Research Strategies: Finding the Right Sources.* Fact Finders. Mankato, MN: Capstone Press, 2013.

Asselin, Kristine Carlson. *Think for Yourself: Avoiding Plagiarism.* Fact Finders. Mankato, MN: Capstone Press, 2013.

Loewen, Nancy. *Just the Facts: Writing Your Own Research Report.* Writer's Toolbox. Mankato, MN: Picture Window Books, 2009.

WEBSITES

For an excellent interactive guide to research, check out this site: www.kyvl.org/kids/homebase.html

Improve your Internet researching skills by reading this site: www.kidscomputerlab.org/index.php/research-skills

This site provides five ways to make research easier: kidshealth.org/teen/school_jobs/school/online_research.html

Publisher's note to educators and parents: Our editors have carefully reviewed these websites to ensure that they are suitable for students. Many websites change frequently, however, and we cannot guarantee that a site's future contents will continue to meet our high standards of quality and educational value. Be advised that students should be closely supervised whenever they access the Internet.

INDEX

atlases 12

background reading 8–9
bibliography 27
books 5, 6, 11, 12–13, 14–15, 18,
   19, 20, 23, 26, 27
brainstorming 8–9

chapters 14, 15, 21
contents, table of 14
crediting 26–27

dictionaries 12
domain names 18
drawings 6

encyclopedias 5, 9, 11, 12

illustrations 15, 21
index cards 25, 29
indexes 14, 15
Internet 4, 5, 16–17, 18–19, 23,
   26, 27
interviews 6, 10, 11

journals 6

key words 7, 9, 17, 20

librarians 12, 13
libraries 5, 13, 14, 16, 18

magazines 4, 11, 26
mindmaps 9

newspapers 4, 11, 26
note-taking 4, 5, 22–23, 24–25, 26,
   27, 28, 29

outlines 7, 28, 29

photographs 6, 10, 15, 21
plagiarism 27
PowerPoint 6
primary sources 10, 11, 16

questions 5, 7, 11
quotes 6, 23, 29

scanning 20
search engines 16–17
secondary sources 10, 11, 16
skimming 20, 21, 28
spider diagrams 9
surveys 11

topics 6, 7, 8, 9, 11, 12, 13, 15, 16,
   19, 21, 25

video clips 6, 10